199 Fun Writing Prompts

For 4th and 5th Graders

Linda Chiara

Dear Parents and Educators

With these 199 writing prompts, I hope to offer your 4th and 5th graders a jumping-off point to generate ideas, organize their thoughts and express their emotions on paper.

While some prompts are aimed at helping them improve their critical thinking skills and develop thoughtful responses, many others are simply designed to entertain and let them have fun and write freely.

As the author of this book, I understand that choosing the right resources to support your child's and student's education can be a daunting task. That's why positive feedback from readers like you who have found the book helpful is incredibly valuable. Your review can serve as a testament to the quality and effectiveness of the book, and help other parents and educators make an informed decision about whether or not it is the right fit for their needs.

I sincerely hope that your youngsters enjoy these writing prompts!

Contents

1. Creative Writing Prompts   1

2. Family Writing Prompts   18

3. Holidays Writing Prompts   24

4. Music Writing Prompts   29

5. Pets, Animals, and Bugs Writing Prompts   34

About Linda   41

Creative Writing Prompts

1. You have been invited to create a new Superhero comic book series. What type of hero would you create? What would his or her super powers be? Don't forget to include a description of the new villain you'd also be creating for the series.

2. Use this line to either start or finish a story: "I never thought my science experiment would turn my hair green for a whole month!"

3. Which of the following inventions could you not live without: a cell phone, air conditioning, heater, refrigerator, car?

4. Describe the color yellow to a person who is blind.

5. It's your first baseball game of the season and you're up at bat. You're so excited. But suddenly, the opposing team brings out their new star pitcher. To your surprise, it's an octopus with six arms! What happens next?

6. Pretend your classroom has feelings like a person does. Do you think it's happy or sad when the school day ends? Do you think it can't wait for summer vacation to start or do you think it would miss the children too much?

7. Write a story about a picnic from an ant's point of view.

8. One morning you wake up and go to your bedroom window to look out. But you can't see anything because you've been snowed in! The only problem is it's the middle of July. What happened and what are you going to do?

9. Write a story where the LAST line is "And that's how McHenry the rabbit became the star of the show."

10. What do you think the expression *the squeaky wheel gets the grease means*? Write an essay about someone you know who might be considered "a squeaky wheel."

11. You wake up one morning only to find that the year is 1863 and you are in the White House with President Lincoln. What do you tell him about the future of this country?

12. You are having a nightmare where dinosaurs are chasing you. When you wake up you are afraid for a minute to open your eyes. Finally, you summon up the courage to take a peek and when you do you couldn't be more surprised. There standing in your bedroom is...

13. Pick five items that you think would be important to include in a time capsule that will be opened in 100 years from now. What did you pick and why?

14. You've heard the expression *money doesn't grow on trees*. One night before bed, just for fun, you plant a quarter in the yard and the next morning you discover a money tree. What would you do?

15. You are given a reading assignment by your teacher. You must pick one of two books to read. Would you rather read the book about the adventures of an octopus who wants to buy socks for his eight tentacles or a book on the adventures of the dog who flew to the moon? Why did you pick the book you did and what type of adventures do you think the characters in the book you picked had?

16. You opened up a fortune cookie and read an unusual fortune. The next morning the fortune comes true. Write about what happened.

17. One morning you wake up and discover that you are trapped inside of a snow globe. How do you get out?

18. What one word describes your best friend? Why did you pick that word?

19. Explain what the expression *people who live in glass houses shouldn't throw stones* means.

20. The garden you planted in the spring has grown wild. The flowers grew up the side of the house and are now creeping in through your bedroom window. However, each time you try to cut them back, they grow twice as fast and twice as tall. In fact, it's gotten so bad, your parents think you are going to have to move! But who would buy a house where the flowers are taking over? Think about, then write about, what you can do to solve the problem.

21. Sometimes we surprise ourselves with what we're able to do. Write a story about a time you accomplished something you didn't think you could.

22. Superheroes, like Spiderman, don't use weapons to subdue their enemies. Instead, they rely on a few special tools and their own resourcefulness. Describe a time when you saved the day with your quick thinking.

23. What do you think the expression *lie down with dogs, wake up with fleas* means?

24. "If only I had wings," you said as you looked at the mess before you. "Then I could fly away from all of this." Where are you, what type of mess are you looking at, and how did it get that way?

25. Just once I wish my mom wouldn't...

26. Children from the country of Chad in Africa do not celebrate birthdays. That being said, pretend you have a new student in your class who has just arrived from Chad and whose birthday is in three weeks. How would you describe the American tradition of big parties and lots of presents to a child who has never had even a small party? Would you plan a surprise celebration for him?

27. Your younger sister will be starting kindergarten soon and she is nervous about going. Write a list of things you want to tell her about what you do in kindergarten. Give examples of your experiences when you went to school for the first time.

28. On your way home from school one day, you find a magic talking rock. It tells you that you will be granted your heart's desire, but first, however, you must complete one really difficult task. What is your heart's desire and what do you have to do to earn it?

29. You want to write a message in a bottle and toss it into the ocean. What would you write as your message?

30. You just made a new friend with someone who has never tasted pizza before. Using descriptive words, describe to her how it looks, smells, feels in your hands, and tastes.

31. Your parents have said you can have a new scooter, but you need to pay for part of it with your own money which you've earned. Write an essay explaining what you can do to earn the money.

32. As we grow older, we take on more responsibility. Write about a time when you were given a responsibility that you were not ready for.

33. Think of a story using these words: tumble, mirror, crow, toothbrush and helicopter.

34. You like scary movies, your best friend likes comedies. Your parents are taking you to the movies this weekend. How do you decide what type of movie you'll see?

35. Have you ever tried a new food that you were absolutely, positively sure you would hate, only to find that you liked it? Write about the food and what you thought it was going to taste like.

36. Using your knowledge of your local geography and environment, explain to a new inhabitant how to find your favorite pizza restaurant in your town.

37. Write an essay explaining what you think the expression *a fool and his money are soon parted* means.

38. The mess in your bedroom is out of control. Your parents have issued an ultimatum...you get to keep your bed and any other furniture in your room. Other than that you can only keep three items. What items would you keep? Write about what those three items mean to you.

39. What is the world's greatest invention in your opinion? Write a thank letter to the inventor of your favorite invention.

40. Instead of ketchup, mustard, onions, relish, pickles or even sauerkraut, you need to create a whole new set of toppings for a hot dog. What creative and flavorful toppings would you like to see on a hot dog?

41. Your mom was baking her famous chocolate chip, animal cracker, banana nut cake, but something went terribly wrong. What happened to the cake and what does it taste like?

42. If you had the chance to perform in a talent show, what would you do? What is one of your talents?

43. Rewrite the story of Cinderella from one of the wicked step-sister's point of view.

44. Describe what strawberries smell like.

45. Write a short story that has these words in it: thunderstorm, piano, sunglasses, hotdog, gorilla.

46. Do you think it would be fun sometimes to be an only child? Why or why not? If you are already an only child, what do you love or dislike about it?

47. Your cousin is moving to your town. Write a letter explaining why your town is such a wonderful place to live.

48. Something happened on a Wednesday that now makes Wednesdays your least favorite day of the week. What happened?

49. What was your favorite TV show when you were in kindergarten? Do you think if you watched the same show now, four or five years later, you would still find it as interesting as you did then? Why or why not?

50. Rewrite the story of Goldilocks and The Three Bears from Mama Bear's point of view.

51. Your friends have a nickname for you. They call you Blizzard. How did you get that name?

52. If you had to give up pizza, hotdogs, hamburger, or candy for one year, which would you choose?

53. There's an expression which states, *he can't see the* *forest for the trees*. Write a paragraph explaining what you think that expression means.

54. Write a poem about the joys (the beach) and the perils (mosquitoes) of summer.

55. You wake up one morning and find that both you and your kitten have shrunk down to the size of butterflies. Write a story about your adventures.

56. Today you're the backpack of a first grader. Describe the adventures of your day.

57. As soon as I looked at my test grade, I knew I'd never get to...

58. You're in an elevator with the one person in the world that you really dislike. Suddenly the elevator gets stuck between floors. Write a story in which you two become friends by the time you are rescued. Use lots of dialogue for this one!

59. Explain something that is hard for you to do.

60. You won a stuffed rabbit at the town's local carnival. When you get it home, you find that he can walk and talk! What kind of adventures do you have together?

61. How would you describe the sound of a tuba to someone who is deaf?

62. After a big picnic lunch on the fourth of July, you take a nap on a blanket. When you wake up, it's snowing. What happened? Did you sleep into winter like Rip Van Winkle or is it a surprise summer snow storm?

63. What one thing are you proud to have mastered?

64. You get to change places with someone for one week. Who would you like to change places with? How do you think your life would be different for that week?

65 You're in the movie theater with your parents watching a Pixar movie, when all of a sudden you find yourself as one of the characters in the movie. What movie were you watching and what character did you become? Write a story about how it feels to be in the movie.

66. You have a choice. You can either be the best singer in the world or the best doctor. Which do you choose and why?

67. Today you get to create a new pizza. The toppings on your pizza must match a theme. For example, only round foods, or only yellow foods, or even only spicy foods. What theme will you pick and what toppings will you choose?

68. If you had to change your name, what name would you pick as your new name?

69. You have the chance to change the colors of the world around you for one day only. Just for today, the sky doesn't have to be blue, the grass doesn't have to be green and snow doesn't have to be white. What colors would you pick for the world around you and why?

70. How do you feel about rainy days? Do you like them because everything feels fresh afterwards and you like a day of coziness and laziness? Or do they make you sad because you are one of those people who needs the sun to be shining to feel happy inside?

71. Write a story with this opening..."Once upon a time in a land called Trop, there lived 3 tropkolopes. Their names were..._____, _____, and _____". What type of creatures are tropkolopes and what happens to them in the land of Trop?

72. You are lucky enough to be in a hot air balloon flying high above everyone. Write a description of all that you see.

73. What is something you've always wanted to ask your mom and dad, but haven't? Why not?

74. Close your eyes and listen. What do you hear? Write about the sounds using descriptive words.

75. Your three-year-old sister is in your room when you come home from school. You look around and all of your toys, stuffed animals, books, even your bed is covered with red marker. Write a story about how you feel and how you handle the situation.

76. If you could eat only one meal every night, what would it be?

77. Start a story with this opening. "It was raining the day I rode my bike to ……."

78. If I told you once I've told you a thousand times," Coach Munson said, "You're never going to make it if you don't…."

79. The headline of your local newspaper reads MAN DIGS UP TREASURE IN HIS OWN BACKYARD! Write the newspaper article that accompanies it. Be sure to mention why he was digging in the first place and what he found.

80. Imagine you had the power to go back to any time in your life and change one thing. What would you change and why?

81. Write a story about how the zebra got his stripes.

82. You can only eat one fruit from this list for the rest of your life: grapes, apples, oranges, peaches, plums, watermelon or banana. Which fruit would you pick? Do you think you'd get tired of it after a year?

83. Explain what the expression *his bark is worse than his bite means*. Did you ever meet someone that fits this description? Write a story about it.

84. Your mother just came home with a dresser for your room that she bought at a tag sale. When you look inside the drawers, you find a hidden letter which has yellowed from age. What did the letter say and who wrote it?

85. I knew the second I woke up today that this day was going to be a disaster. And it's all because of...

86. Imagine you are climbing on the jungle gym and you slip and fall. Instead of hitting the ground, you flap your arms and start to fly. What happens next?

87. Every day at exactly at 2:00, the elderly lady who lives across the street from you goes into her garden, looks up at the sky and sings a song from an opera. Write a short story about who she is and why she does that.

88. Abracadabra! You know the magic word to immediately transport yourself somewhere else. Where would you like to be at this very moment and why did you choose that place?

89. You've been told a thousand times, never, never go down to the basement. It was totally off limits. However, today you're home alone. You sneak down the stairs and discover...

90. Write about three foods that you wouldn't touch with a 10-foot pole and why.

91. What are your favorite types of books to read? Do you prefer fiction or non-fiction? Why did you choose the one you did?

92. There's a big snowstorm that has knocked out all of your electricity. That means no cooking, no watching TV or using any other electronic device, and no heat or lights. What are you going to do all day and how are you going to stay warm? What will you eat?

93. Close your eyes for a few seconds and then open

them. What is the first thing you saw. Write a paragraph describing it.

94. Imagine that you get to sit down with three former presidents (either living or dead) and talk to them. What three would you pick and what would you say to them?

95. What kind of day makes you happiest? Describe what you would do if you had a whole day to yourself to do whatever it is you love.

96. You decide that cleaning is a waste of time and you decide not to clean your room at all. Describe what your room would look like after one week. How would it look after a month? A year?

97. If it rained for month and you couldn't play outdoors, what would you do to make sure you won't be bored? Make a list of things you can do to entertain yourself indoors.

98. Rank the days of the week in order from your favorite day to your least favorite. Why did you put them in the order that you did?

99. You're exploring a cave when you find a staircase that looks like it leads deep into the underground. Write about what happens next.

Family Writing Prompts

1. There's Mother's Day, Father's Day, Grandparent's Day and Sibling Day. Should there also be a Kid's Day? Why or why not? If a Kid's Day is decreed, how do you think it should be celebrated?

2. Your brother or sister is having a birthday. Your grandparents have asked for ideas for a present. Write a letter to them suggesting several gifts for your sibling and explain why these gifts are a good choice.

3. Where are you in the family tree? Are you the oldest, middle, youngest, or an only child? Write an essay explaining the advantages of your special position in the family. Or write an essay explaining which position you would prefer to be and why.

4. Manners have changed over the course of time. For example, texting at the dinner table was unheard of several years ago, and writing a thank you note for a gift was considered the norm. Describe the differences in the manners your parents were taught compared to what you were taught.

5. Imagine that you could "invent" the perfect sibling. What would this dream brother or sister be like? Write a description.

6. Tell about a time your family ate a special meal together. Be sure to describe the environment, the food, the sounds and more.

7. Think of a time you were on a car trip with your family and describe the trip. Think about the demeanor of those in the car, the things you did to pass the time, the scenery, the car itself and more.

8. Visualize someone in your family and describe them in detail.

9. Write a story about how you and one of your parents, grandparents or a particular family member interact together, and how the bond has affected your life in positive ways.

10. For your vacation this year, your parents have laid out three options for you. You can either go on an African Safari, or visit a castle in England, or you can go to a dude ranch in Montana and ride in a covered wagon. Which do you prefer and why?

11. Think of a family member who is the most influential in your life and describe the traits that make them such an important person.

12. Write an essay about your most unusual relative. What unusual thing has he or she done? Is this person well known outside of your family for this accomplishment?

13. Many children have jobs or chores to do to help out at home. Think about a job you have and explain why it is important for your family. If you don't do your job, does it impact someone else?

14. Do you have a friend that your parents are not so fond of? Why is that? Can you look at the situation from your parents' point of view?

15. Does your family use labels to describe you and your siblings? Is one of you the athletic one, the musical one, the bookworm? Do you agree with the labels assigned to each of you? Do you think parents should use labels to describe their children? Why or why not?

16. When parents set limits and discipline their children, they often say, "Someday, you'll understand why I'm doing this." Write about a time when you realized that your parents were doing what they thought was best, even though it made you very angry at the time.

17. You are in charge of the fun for the weekend with your family. Would you prefer to do an outdoor activity like the park or the zoo? Or would you rather stay home and watch a movie or play board games?

18. This year your family has decided to have a "stay-cation" rather than a traditional vacation. That means you will have a local vacation; you will stay in your own neighborhood. What types of things can you do locally? Does your town have certain celebrations? Can you plan on a backyard camp-out or do you have a bowling alley near by? What would be your idea of a perfect "stay-cation"?

19. Your parents played a game of pin the tail on the donkey, only instead of a donkey they pinned a world map to decide where you would vacation this year. The pin landed on Morocco! What do you think are the types of things you can do in Morocco? What types of clothes will you need to pack? If you don't know anything at all about the country, write your essay and then look Morocco up to see if you were even close in what you think it would be like.

20. With the hope of learning more about and preserving your family's history, describe the kind of questions you would ask an older relative.

21. What physical traits do you share with a family member?

22. Write about how your parents met. If you don't know how they met, make something up!

23. Imagine that you are able to invite one person from history for dinner one night with you and your family. Who would you invite? Why did you choose that person?

24. You can only keep one memory from your childhood.

What memory would that be?

25. Are you related to anyone famous, either living or dead? If so, who are you related to, and is it something your family likes to share with others, or is it considered a taboo subject in your house?

Holidays Writing Prompts

1. Lucky you! You get to create a new holiday! And it can be as fun or silly or as serious as you like. What type of holiday will you create? What will the traditions be? Will there be special food associated with it? Will gifts be involved?

2. In England they celebrate Guy Fawkes Day with a bonfire on November 5th each year. Research and write about the holiday.

3. One holiday is going to be eliminated from the calendar this year and you are the one who has to choose it. Which holiday would you pick and why?

4. The first Friday each October we celebrate World's Smile Day, represented by the popular yellow smiley face. The holiday became so popular that the U.S. Post Office issued a stamp with the smiley face. The holiday offers an opportunity to extend an act of kindness. Write about an act of kindness you will perform on the next World Smile Day!

5. Ramadan is the Islamic holiday that runs annually for one month. One of the observances of the holiday is to fast (not eat anything at all) from sunrise to sunset. One of the many reasons Muslims fast during the holiday is to help them understand the plight of the poor. Do you think you would be able to fast every day during the day for thirty days in a row? Do you think there are other ways to teach empathy about the less fortunate? If you don't think you'd be able to fast, what could you do to help you understand the sufferings of the poor?

6. Describe what you think would be a perfect birthday party.

7. We celebrate our veterans on two separate holidays each year. The holidays are Memorial Day in May and Veteran's Day in November. Research what the difference is between the two holidays and write an essay on what those differences are.

8. Imagine you're using cookie cutters to bake Christmas cookies. All of a sudden, the reindeer cookies and the gingerbread cookies come alive! What happens next?

9. Every September on the 4th Friday of the month we celebrate Native American Day. This special holiday dates back to 1939. Write an essay explaining how your town could help bring more awareness to this little known holiday.

10. December 16 is National Chocolate Covered Anything Day and to celebrate your friend gives you a chocolate covered grasshopper. Explain whether you would eat it or not, and why.

11. Many people celebrate holidays which are particular to their culture, such as Saint Patrick's Day for the Irish, Oktoberfest for Germany and Cinco de Mayo for Mexico. Does your family celebrate an unusual or culturally significant holiday? Write about it if you do!

12. Write a story about your favorite Halloween

costume.

13. Not every country around the world celebrates birthdays. Vietnam, China and some countries in Africa don't mark the anniversary of one's birth. How do you feel about that? Should your birthday be cause for a celebration? Do we overdo birthdays in this country with big parties and extravagant gifts? Write an essay expressing your view on birthdays.

14. Many people decorate their houses in different ways for the holidays. Write about how you decorate your home.

15. How would you improve your town's Halloween celebrations?

16. October 15 is National Grouch Day. Do you know someone who is perpetually grouchy? How do you feel when you spend time with that person?

17. Presidents are usually the one people to get a national holiday for their birthday. However, Martin Luther King, Jr. was never the president, yet we have a national holiday to honor him. What did he do to deserve this honor?

18. On December 8th we celebrate Rosa Parks Day. We

all know that it is wrong to break the law. Rosa Parks broke the law and went to jail. The law she broke was to refuse to give her bus seat to a white man. Was that a fair law? What should we do if a law is unfair?

19. Write a story about a groundhog who refuses to get out of his warm bed to do his prediction, so winter never ends. Can you write a story with a happy ending? Or is everyone doomed to be cold forever?

20. August 13th is National Left Handers Day. The holiday was created to bring awareness to how difficult some things are for left handed people. For example, if you are left handed, you'll find that scissors and spiral notebooks are designed for right handed people. On National Left Handers Day, you are required to do everything left handed. Do you think you could do it? What difficulties to you think you'd encounter? Write an essay imagining a day of being left handed.

21. March 8th is the International Woman's Day. Write an essay about a woman you admire. It could be your mother, a teacher, a neighbor, or anyone famous.

Music Writing Prompts

1. What's more important in a song in your opinion, the music or the lyrics? Why?

2. Which instrument do you think is more difficult to learn? Playing piano, playing guitar, or playing the trumpet? Which did you choose and why?

3. A famous musician once said that the reason he loved the banjo so much was because you can't play a sad tune on it. Are there any other instruments that you can think of that can only play happy, uplifting music? If you can't think of one, write about why you think the banjo has that one special quality.

4. Think of your favorite movie. Now imagine if it had no music in it. Would it still be your favorite movie? What kind of impact does music have in a movie?

5. Do you play a musical instrument? Why did you choose the instrument you did? If you don't play one, which one would you like to play? Why did you pick the one you did?

6. What's the first song you remember learning as a child? Who taught it to you? Do you still remember the words and music?

7. Pick a favorite line from a favorite song and write about what it means to you personally.

8. Listen to a song in a language you are not familiar with. Do you understand the mood of the song without knowing the words?

9. The new school you moved to thinks that music is a waste of time. There are no music classes, no choir classes, no music played at sports events, and no one is allowed to listen to music on their electronic devices while on school grounds or on the bus. How do you think that will affect the mood of the students?

10. Is there a song that makes you happy every time you hear it? Write about it and why it affects you that way.

11. There are five main instrument families: keyboards, strings, brass, woodwind and percussion. If you could play one instrument from each family type, which five instruments would you play and why?

12. Think about your favorite singer, band or musician and write a letter to a friend from another country telling about this musician and why he or she is your favorite.

13. Your music teacher has asked you to research three unusual instruments and pick the one you'd like to learn to play. The instruments are a tsabouna, a tamburitza and a kazoo. After researching the instruments, write an essay explaining why you chose the one you did.

14. Make up a song about a dancing frog and a guitar playing crocodile. What would the song be about?

15. Choose a specific establishment (shopping mall, law firm, doctor's office, sports stadium, fast food restaurant, fine dining establishment) and imagine you were in charge of choosing the music for it. Explain how music can affect one's mood. Explain what type of music you'll use and why.

16. There's been studies done that showed that college students who listened to a sonata by Mozart for a few minutes before taking a test did better than students who listened to no music or even music by another musician. Do you believe that music can make you more intelligent just by listening to it? Should teachers play Mozart sonatas whenever they give a test?

17. What's the first song you remember learning when you were in preschool? Who taught it to you? Do you still remember the words and music?

18. If Beethoven came back to life today and heard his music being used to sell everything from cars to diapers, do you think he'd be happy that his music had reached such a wide audience or do you think he'd be disgusted that the music he worked on for so long was used in advertising?

19. Picture yourself deep in the woods. Can you visualize the sounds that are being made by the birds, the breezes in the trees, the small animals scurrying around? Does it sound like music to you?

20. Music can get your heart racing or help calm you down. Think of a song which does either of these and write how it makes you feel when you listen to it. Why do you think it affects you the way it does.

21. Do you think that the saying, "Music is a language that everyone understands" is true? Why or why not?

Pets, Animals, and Bugs Writing Prompts

1. Imagine you are a dog. Only you're no ordinary dog. You are a dog with wings! Describe what your days would be like.

2. Pretend you're a bird sitting up high in a tree. Describe in detail what you see and how things look to you.

3. The town of Churchill in northern Manitoba, Canada, is considered the polar bear capital of the world. It's not uncommon for a polar bear to come down and roam the streets. For this reason, residents of Churchill keep the door to their houses and cars unlocked, in case someone needs to escape a polar bear. Pretend you went up to Churchill for a visit, and suddenly found yourself being chased by a polar bear. Write an essay about your scary adventure!

4. Do bees have ears?

5. Today is Answer an Elephant's Question day. An elephant is going to ask you a question and you are to answer it. What kind of a question do you think an elephant would ask?

6. Describe a bird, an insect, or animal that you have strong feelings about. For example, choose one that scares, amuses, or puzzles you. Research the animal well enough so that you can describe it fully. Use sensory details that will make your classmates feel the same.

7. Make up a new animal. Describe the important features of the animal; for example, what it looks like, and where it lives. Write from the viewpoint of the first person to discover this animal.

8. Write a story with the title, "The Year The Easter Bunny and The Groundhog Changed Jobs".

9. Would you rather look like a rooster or smell like a skunk?

10. Write a story about the day Harvey the sloth raced Freddie the turtle around the high school track. Who won and how long did the race last?

11. Sharks can regrow teeth throughout their lifetimes. The time it takes for a shark to regrow a tooth can vary from a few days to a few months. Imagine if scientists can figure out how it's possible for sharks to do this, and then apply it to humans. Do you believe that it would be a benefit for humanity?

12. Write an essay about the differences between two different types of insects. Show circumstances on how each type adapts to its environment.

13. Giraffes have long necks, zebras have stripes and elephants have long trunks. Pick one of these animals and write a story about how they got their unusual features.

14. Which would make a better pet for your family? An anteater or a platypus?

15. You are a bee. Write about your typical day and how you deal with any dangers you encounter.

16. Which is the better pet? A dog or a cat? Write an essay giving your view on the pros and cons of owning the animal of your choice.

17. One day you come home from school only to find 100 dogs of all shapes and sizes sitting in your front yard. Write a story about how they got there and what you hope will happen.

18. Write an essay giving your view on the pros and cons of owning either a monkey or a horse. Which would be the better pet? Why?

19. You just found a puppy or kitten all alone in your front yard. Write a letter to your parents explaining why you want to keep it and why you should be allowed to have it. Be sure to include all of the ways you would take care of it and how you would earn the money needed for food and vet bills.

20. Would you like to be a bird? Why or why not? If yes, what type of bird would you want to be?

21. Write an essay about an animal that you can't stand. Why don't you like it? Have you ever had any experience with that type of animal? Could you ever learn to like it?

22. Would you like to have a dog who is as big as a horse? Where would he sleep? How difficult would it be to get him in the car or take him for a walk?

23. You get to be a dog. Would you prefer to be a big dog like a Golden Retriever, a Labrador or a German Shepherd? Or would you prefer to be a cute, cuddly lap dog, like a terrier, a beagle or a dachshund? Why did you make the choice you did?

24. Most scientists believe that warm blooded animals have dreams just like humans do. What do you think a walrus dreams about?

25. Pretend you live in an apartment and your parents have said you can choose any pet you want. You pick a llama! How is your family going to manage living with a llama in an apartment?

26. You are a type of fish. State what type of fish you are. Describe your typical day and how you deal with any dangers you encounter.

27. Animals can sometimes seem incredibly human. Describe an experience with an animal that acted in a very human way.

28. Pretend you are a bee buzzing around. What does the world look like from your point of view? Are you confident because you have a stinger that can save you or are you frightened because you are one of the smaller things on the planet?

29. Snakes slither instead of walk, since they have no legs or feet. Imagine being a snake and waking up one morning to discover you suddenly have feet and legs. What would you do? How would you feel?

30. You are a type of insect. State what type of bug you are and describe your typical day. How do you deal with any dangers you encounter?

31. One day you get home from school earlier than usual. When you open the door your dog seems surprised to see you. But you are the one who is really surprised! Because instead of laying on his dog bed, he's sitting at the computer typing! What happens next?

32. What would happen if all of the animals in the zoo traded places with all of the animals on the farm. Describe how the zookeeper and the farmer would react if that happened.

33. You've entered your dog in the "best looking dog" contest at the local fair. He doesn't win that title, however. Instead, he wins the blue ribbon for being the...

About Linda

I'm an award-winning columnist, author, editor and teacher, who has dedicated a lifetime to the wonderful art of making writing fun. My writings appear in a variety of publications, including *Boys' Life, Christian Home and School, Readers' Digest, Chicken Soup for the Soul,* and *Christian Science Monitor*, as well as in many state standardized testing books, including *Measuring Up to the New York State Learning Standards* and *Measuring Up to the Texas Essential Knowledge and Skills*, among others.

Other of my writing prompts books available on Amazon include:

50 Writing Prompts Activity Book for Your 2nd Grader
https://www.amazon.com/dp/B0C7T3KRXZ
The 50 Writing Prompts Workbook for Your 3rd Grader
https://www.amazon.com/dp/B0C2SD1F79

200 Fun Writing Prompts for Your 6th, 7th and 8th Graders
https://www.amazon.com/dp/B0C9SHK3TN

Writing Prompts for Kids: Thought-Provoking Prompts Based on Quotes from History's Most Famous and Influential Thinkers - Grades 4th - 12th
https://www.amazon.com/dp/B0C6BXW8BM

During these wonderful years I've had the pleasure of raising three young boys, who have since grown into three young men, who have given me the beautiful gift of grandparenthood.

If you've enjoyed this book please consider posting an Amazon review. I'm always happy to hear your comments and suggestions. Please click here for your review – or scan this code below.

SCAN HERE